CELEBRATING THE CITY OF FUKUOKA

Celebrating the City of Fukuoka

Walter the Educator

Silent King Books

Copyright © 2024 by Walter the Educator

All rights reserved. No part of this book may be reproduced in any manner whatsoever without written per- mission except in the case of brief quotations embodied in critical articles and reviews.

First Printing, 2024

Disclaimer

This book is a literary work; the story is not about specific persons, locations, situations, and/or circumstances unless mentioned in a historical context. Any resemblance to real persons, locations, situations, and/or circumstances is coincidental. This book is for entertainment and informational purposes only. The author and publisher offer this information without warranties expressed or implied. No matter the grounds, neither the author nor the publisher will be accountable for any losses, injuries, or other damages caused by the reader's use of this book. The use of this book acknowledges an understanding and acceptance of this disclaimer.

Celebrating the City of Fukuoka is a little collectible souvenir book that belongs to the Celebrating Cities Book Series by Walter the Educator. Collect them all and more books at WaltertheEducator.com

USE THE EXTRA SPACE TO TAKE NOTES AND DOCUMENT YOUR MEMORIES

FUKUOKA

In Fukuoka, where the rivers whisper to the dawn,

Celebrating the City of Fukuoka

Between the mountains' embrace and ocean's endless song,

A city thrives, where history and future intertwine,

In streets adorned with cherry blossoms, and temples so divine.

The sun rises over Hakata Bay, a golden hue it spreads,

Kissing the waves, it wakes the day, while lanterns overhead,

Reflect in shimmering waters, tales of old unfold,

Of samurai and merchants bold, and secrets yet untold.

In Ohori Park, tranquility wraps each soul,

With swans that glide on placid lakes, and gardens that extol,

A harmony of nature, a sanctuary of peace,

Where time slows down, and moments of sheer beauty never cease.

The yatai stands, an evening's delight,

With scents of ramen, sizzling skewers in the night,

A gastronomic paradise, flavors rich and true,

Each bite a story, each dish a rendezvous.

Celebrating the City of Fukuoka

Nanzen-ji's ancient halls, echo with the past,

Silent sentinels of eras gone, their shadows long they cast,

Yet in their stillness, life anew does bloom,

As monks in meditation find solace in each room.

Oh, Fukuoka, city of festivals so grand,

With Koinobori soaring, and Hakata Gion Yamakasa bands,

A celebration of life, of culture deep and wide,

Where every heart beats with pride, and joy cannot hide.

The bustling streets of Tenjin, a symphony of life,

With fashion, art, and music, where innovation is rife,

Yet amidst the modern marvels, tradition holds its ground,

In weaving of the old and new, a unique beauty found.

To Momochi's shores, where futuristic dreams arise,

With towers that touch the heavens, piercing azure skies,

A testament to progress, yet grounded in the earth,

Celebrating the City of Fukuoka

Fukuoka's spirit shines, a beacon of its worth.

In autumn's golden splendor, the mountains dressed in fire,

And winter's cloak of quiet, as snowflakes inspire,

The cycle of the seasons, in perfect harmony,

A dance of nature's wisdom, unfolding gracefully.

And when the cherry blossoms fall, a fleeting blush of spring,

In Maruyama's ancient grove, the songbirds softly sing,

A promise of renewal, a whisper of the past,

In Fukuoka's gentle heart, eternal love is cast.

Celebrating the City of Fukuoka

ABOUT THE CREATOR

Walter the Educator is one of the pseudonyms for Walter Anderson. Formally educated in Chemistry, Business, and Education, he is an educator, an author, a diverse entrepreneur, and he is the son of a disabled war veteran. "Walter the Educator" shares his time between educating and creating. He holds interests and owns several creative projects that entertain, enlighten, enhance, and educate, hoping to inspire and motivate you. Follow, find new works, and stay up to date with Walter the Educator™

at WaltertheEducator.com

Milton Keynes UK
Ingram Content Group UK Ltd.
UKHW021135080824
446563UK00015B/593